Barefootin' the Country

LACEY ARTHUR

Order this book online at www.trafford.com
or email orders@trafford.com

Most Trafford titles are also available at major online book retailers.

Printed in the United States of America.

ISBN: 978-1-4907-2457-7 (sc)
ISBN: 978-1-4907-2458-4 (e)

Trafford rev. 01/13/2014

www.trafford.com

North America & international
toll-free: 1 888 232 4444 (USA & Canada)
fax: 812 355 4082

CONTENTS

"All you need to make it through today
is a little experience from yesterday
and a little hope for tomorrow."

PART I

this road i walk

black and white photos mark the miles
dust burns my eyes rocks hurt my feet
i'll keep walking 'til it turns to gold
through all weather patterns cold or heat

dust dries my eyes rocks cut my feet
there's no pavement on this ole road
shiver through cold sweat through heat
no one can walk this long road for me

there are no signs on this ole road
no lines to guide me through the night
no one can walk this narrow road with me
when curves come up i'll hug them tight

no lines to show which way is right
roads intersect and run parallel to me
none but this one leads to light
when will its end come to set me free

roads may interrupt and mirror me
and color photos will mark the miles
when its end finally sets me free
'cause i kept walking 'til it turned gold

Tomorrow Quatrain

Today's tomorrow's yesterday,
don't run through it in haste,
for yesterday is then a waste
and tomorrow's thrown away.

How should a country girl's worth be measured

Not in terms of her physical beauty
of which she is unaware
but in her belief in virtue
few do share
>   For her beauty
>   natural and unforced
>   as fall leaves carried
>   in a gently flowing stream

Not in terms of her monetary wealth
for which she has no care
but in her acts of benevolence
beyond compare
>   For she gives
>   of herself and time
>   pricelessly imprinted
>   into memories and photographs

Not in terms of her intelligence
so often overlooked
but in her quick wit
intellect overtook
>   For she knows
>   what is implied in "wo"
>   that sets her apart
>   from "man" alone

Not in terms of her good deeds
rarely recognized
but in the bad ones too
is overall goodness sized
>   For she believes
>   there is good and bad
>   in all of us but one
>   will shine true

Fulfillment

Impressions of feet in wet sand.
Short strides occasionally pause
for curious hands to pick up shells
with which the ocean decorates its beaches,
anxious to find something in each one.
Stooping where waves
only reach as high as ankles,
and wash off sand until another step is taken.

Eyes of deep ocean blue,
darkest in center, lightest around edges,
wonder if it is the shell that grows, or just what lives in it.
Shells can change along
with the hands that behold them.
If shaped differently, how they are all related.
Different names and different families,
yet still just a shell like all others.

Eyes of deep ocean blue,
darkest in center, lightest around edges,
admire with raised brow,
how the pastel spectrum came to be,
of pinks, yellows, lavenders,
and the feel under fingertips
of smooth and rough, lines and grids.

Eyes of deep ocean blue,
darkest in center, lightest around edges,
watch as waves bring shells in, take shells out,
and realize with furrowed brow,
that all shells are alike
because they are all different.
Some thin and easily shattered,
some thick and worn away,
some stripped of their colors
and turned to rainy-day gray;
all broken, all chipped, and weathered;
yet through all the rocks, waves, and beaches
most are still just empty shells.

Things We've Learned in College

Sweatpants, wife beaters, and Rainbows
replace slacks, button-downs and heels
      unless you oversleep your 8 am class
      then it's just brush your hair and teeth
      and add a bra in under your pj's.

Makeup is usually optional
according to the individual
      unless it's smeared leftovers from where
      you were out the night before and lacked
      the time and energy to remove or reapply.

Frozen dinners and various forms of takeout and delivery
replace either mom's home cooking or petite salads
      unless your eating disorder continues
      into college so that you look better
      when you "study" at the beach.
Leftover pizza is good at any meal, microwaved or cold,
and easy to grab on your way out the door.

Since you now have to do your own laundry
many clothes are worn more than once
      unless they don't pass the smell test
      then layers is an option depending
      on the degree of smell.

No matter how broke you may get
you can always afford a $4 coffee
      unless you're one of those people
      who are already hyperactive
      and caffeine makes you more annoying.

Those not abiding by these typical rules
are usually trying too hard for extra credit.
The rest of us are simply too smart to care
how fat we look in our bum clothes walking
at least a mile across campus to an 8 am.

Take Me Down

Up here the bright city lights hurt my eyes
cause them to squint until they're nothing
more than thin blue slits over full cheeks.

Take me down to a dirt road beneath green
canopies of foliage through which the sun
peaks in patches of pastel yellow rays.

I never did look good in neon colors anyway
they always made me look pale, washed-out,
transparent, and make-up is just another mask.

Take me down to where the moon follows me
no matter how many turns I take down roads
and I no longer have to search for its glow.

It still takes me a while to get to sleep here
with the cacophony of incessant traffic
mixture of horns, squealing breaks, sirens.

Take me down to where the crickets sing
me to sleep at night and the birds sing me
awake in morning with their melodies.

In the daytime when the lights are off
everything seems gray, very little green
it's all just concrete and buildings.

Take me down to lie in beds of clover
let the wind sprinkle my hair with
rainbow spectrum petals of wildflowers.

I've become accustomed to strange looks
for how I talk or dress, they just nod a fake
smile with stereotypical understanding.

Take me down to open pastures to run wild
while rain cascades about me and no one
thinks I'm crazy for not having an umbrella.

I was taught from the Bible to love your
neighbors but here I don't even know
their names, just cars and a few faces.

Take me down to where everyone appreciates
where I've come from, who I am, and believes
in me for where I'm going, hoping I'll return.

I'm here to learn I say but life educates more
than schools, and familiarizing the unfamiliar,
appreciating the familiar more than books.

Lord, please take me down until you come
don't let me grow and learn so much
that I forget to love where I'm from.

It's Only Me Again

Hello, it's only me again.
Do you recognize my voice?
I have some questions for you.
You rarely take the time to answer
      when I call you anymore.

No, I'm not trying to sell anything,
      what I have for you is free.
Besides, I have more riches
      than a man can imagine.

When did I go from the one
      you'd call others back for
      to the one you put on hold
      when someone else calls

When did I go from the one
      you told everything to
      to the one you only call
      when something goes wrong

What happened to the times
      we walked side by side
Now you try to walk ahead alone
      instead of waiting for me.

I've held your hand through lions
      dens of deceit, deserts of loneliness,
      and fiery furnaces of guilt.
I'll still hold your hand when you let go.

What happened to the nights you'd lie
     awake while I wiped your tears
Now you hide your face from me
     and cry into your pillow.

What would you say if I told you
     I'll always love you
Would you say it back, shrug
     it off, or simply walk away.

What would you do if I said
     I'd gladly die for you
Oh yeah, I guess you forgot,
     I already did a long time ago.

My free gift you don't think you need
     I'll not offer it to you again,
You must ask me if you want it,
     I'll be waiting with it.

Goodbye now, this could be me
calling you for the last time.
Maybe you know my voice now.
I hope I've presented you
     with the answers you need.

Question of Eternity

We never learned if sin was partly planned
for it was Lucifer who fell from grace
to earth to tempt and test the human race.
If envy was his sin then it began

with him in heaven not on earth with man.
Instead we learned the serpent brought disgrace
now seen in ev'ry generation's face.
I guess we'll never know until we can

for once and all approach the throne and ask
with face so close to golden ground and tears
from face to feet that only His could be

the He who died the death fulfilled the task
and saved who came to ask in final year.
How will He feel if then we still can't see?

in the Potter's hands

What can I make you?
the old man said as he cut
the clay with string.
I heard it splant onto
the wheel as it turned.
He sprinkled it with water,
to soften it up, he explained.
The squeaking of the pedal
blended with the song
he sang that drowned out
the Mum Festival's crowd.
I watched and listened
as I held a paper headband
that read "Future Doctor",
a gift at another booth.

He's still working on me
to make me what I ought to be . . .

I watched as he kneaded
the clay as one would dough
and picked up the scrap pieces
to add them to the whole.
Crumbs count too, he said.

I looked around at his work,
all the vases, bowls, plates,
cups, and several types
of ash trays in various colors.
Most were finished except
for those in a box set aside.
It was full of cracked, broken,
or unfinished pieces.
Just need more time and patience.

Some had been heated too long,
some had been handled wrong.

I know just what I need to make you,
he said and from a shapeless lump
came a beautiful pitcher in those
sagacious hands. It took much heat
to make it hold its form and many
coats of paint to get it the dark red
he thought that it should be.
He said to come back if there
were ever any problems.
When I asked how much he said,
It's free for you to pour
out life to anyone in need.

Help Me

I walked through house
wares beside toys, looking
for anything I might need
as the auctioneer's voice
radiated through the busy
flea market blending in
with the smoked smell
of barbequed pork plates.
It was almost a tradition to go
to the annual volunteer fire
department sale in Trenton.
Help me, was all I heard
him say amidst the clutter
and chaos of the crowd.
At first I thought he was lost
as I looked into two pools
of dark chocolate, pleading,
until I noticed strawberry
blonde hair stretched thin
over splotched pink skin.
I've never seen sunburn
in the early part of January.
I wasn't in my white coat
today, but I'd seen the same
effects before, only not yet
in a child. But I knew
I had to learn to face it
if I was to pursue the career.

So the truth pulled me down
to his height. I reached out
to hold his hand and tell him
that I'll do my best, I need
more time to finish school,
but at the sound of his name
—Charlie—he was gone.
I lost him down a dead end
aisle, and when I asked
no one else had seen him.

Rain

a
single
drop of rain
fell from the sky
upon her cheek to
become a single tear
her dried up eyes could
not shed for time was
the sun that dried up
sorrow's rain

Dear You,

I know things before you do,
that all those temporary "he's"
were not right for you,
with their shallow flatteries and hollow promises
of worldly traits and treasures
that only appeal to the eyes
and never reach the soul.
I wish I could have prevented
the tears they brought
that froze your heart.
Tears you shed only on me.

I knew you loved the right one
before you would admit it.
The "he" who followed the tears with kisses
from lips whose honesty melted your heart.
With "him" you find the comfort
of watching the sun rise and set
in eyes that reflect only your face.
I knew "he'd" bring happy words
through your hands
that trembled with excitement.

Once you've finally admitted
everything time permits,
my pages full of confessions
that bind us together,
what will you do with me?
Will you rid yourself of me,
rip or shred me into pieces,
toss or hide me away in a box,
replace me with "him",
or carry me throughout your days?

Yellow

blanket
Mama and Granny knitted
when they found out
I was on the way.
Wrapped me in it to carry
me home from the hospital.
1985, when I was born.

teddy bear
named B-bear.
Mama would wind
his music box
and sing me to sleep
with the "Teddy Bear Song".
1986, when I was one.

dress
I wore at Peepaw's funeral.
I can still remember
he did not look like himself,
mouth closed, his lips taunt,
stretched thin like a rubber band.
1988, when I was three.

softballs
I threw to Daddy sitting
on a bucket forty feet away.
Catching and giving signals,
teaching me command
of five different pitches.
1999, when I was fourteen.

rose
I placed on Granny's casket,
while Mama read a poem
about her and her favorite flower.
We planted some
around her headstone.
2000, when I was fifteen.

streaks
I put in my hair
when Daddy said no.
We didn't talk for a week.
Mama didn't see any harm
and gave me the money.
2002, when I was seventeen.

flecks
in Bryan's brown eyes
I learned to love,
prom night dancing
in the yellow headlights,
singing to each other.
2003, when I was eighteen.

golden ring
with a diamond, Bryan gave me
our anniversary, a symbol
of a promise to be fulfilled
before family, friends, and God
one yellow day by the river.
2005, when I was twenty.

PART II

I never asked for a Romeo

I never asked
for a Romeo
'cause I surely
ain't a Juliet,
I'd rather just
have a cowboy
to show me
a red sunset.
He would never
have to climb a tree
to see my face
in moonlight,
or have to toss
pebbles up at
my window's glass
'cause my room
has always been
in reach of grass.

Rising River

A sleepy southern town,
its heart pierced by a river
that rose without rain.
Science held no explanation,
but the old folks said
it overflowed with the tears
two lonely hearts never shed.

For reasons passed through time,
the two sides of the river never mixed.
Unwritten laws forbade
matrimonial union.
Disobedience bore fear
that the river would cry out in rage
and bring death to both sides.

The night of lovers' day,
the river drew two lonely hearts
to each of its edges
for a midnight swim.
Its surface reflecting the stars, moon,
and the separate shadows
of a single silhouette.

It is the bitter-sweet forbidden fruit
that is the most compelling and alluring.
love held captive by loneliness released
by the unspoken sin of a blessed union.
A sin to be their mortal last
far as their loved ones knew.
Their bodies never found and assumed gone,
lost to the river's swells forever.
Now together they love and live,
where the river rises no more.

If It Wasn't for You

I could give other guys more
                        than just one look
            return gestures
                        instead of just a smile
            say yes
                        to dinner invitations
Or dangle more than one
                        on a long thin line
I could have more late nights
                        filing high heels down
                        with easily forgotten strangers
            have a collection
                        of whiskey-ring stained
                        napkins with never-dialed numbers
I would have more time
                        to read books
                        or play an instrument
            more choice
                        in the restaurant where I eat
                              movie I want to see
                              music I want to hear in the car
                              clothes I wear out
I wouldn't know what it was like
                        to dance in headlights
                        swim at the base of a waterfall
Or hike three miles up a mountain
                        breathless at the view from the top
I would have never walked down the beach
                              late at night guided only by the stars
                              and a hand

written
> any more poetry for fear
> of it all becoming fake

had the guts
> to let anyone hear me sing

known what it was like
> to smile and cry at
> just the thought of someone

thought that I
> could ever be
> the woman you see in me

The Farmer's Son and Welder's Daughter

I once thought I had planned my life before
I met someone who saved me from myself.
Relationships were never real because
I would not let them be. I wanted more
than words alone could hold. I had a dream
much bigger than the town I'm from. For it
is here that welders' daughters can't become
the doctors. Here it is that farmers' sons
can just be farmers. My confining plans
I made for life had caused a hunger for
success and left no room for love. I thought
I could just wait to meet my prince, ignore
the frogs until one night he came to me
in jeans, a T-shirt, faded camo hat.
He smiled, and I just couldn't help but smile
right back at him. I was obsessed with love
and yet afraid to give my heart to him
to break and throw away as many did
before I learned to trust. Who would have thought
a farmer's son should be the one to set
this welder's daughter free. He held me close
enough to break me, but I knew that he
could never hurt me. That is what his eyes
conveyed. His hands though tough from work portrayed
a gentle touch which I can but describe
as callused hands that since have turned from rough
to velvet. I am now convinced he must
be crazy when he says that now I'm his
new hero 'cause his mother died a year
before we met of cancer, and that's what
my specialty will be. He thinks I am

so stubborn though, like when I wouldn't say
I love you back to him until it was
the second time I heard it from his lips.
These past few years have taught me that he must
just like my ways because he simply smiles,
shakes his head and kisses me on my nose.
A glittery glint in golden band shows
I know I love him and I tell him so.

Hop-Scotch to Tomorrow

6:45 am cacophony
      uncradling Chihuahua at my feet

I really hope he's not mad at me

caffeine compound of cream and sugar consumed
      unnumbing extremities
      sparkling sapphires
            like sun on ocean depths

I wonder what made him say that

toasted honey wheat English muffin and peanut butter feast
      choking down in 5 minutes

He has no reason not to trust me

hygiene necessities complete
      spinning silk
      polishing pearls

I never should have let him worry

20 minute 6 mile ride
15 minute 1 mile walk

How was I supposed to know my ex would call

words from books
      too expensive to buy
      too heavy to carry
      too hard to read
dictated from a low hum
      in a dark room of 200
people occasionally catching
      their heads mid-fall

Even if my ex was in town

17 credits for 23 hours spent each week
        studying between each lecture and lab

I never had any intention of meeting my ex

6 pounds of fur
        wagging tail
        squeaking toys

It's not like it was a bad break-up

open books and blank pages wait
        soon no longer unread and unwritten

We were going to try to stay friends

leather gloves and weights heavier than yesterday's
        wait to be lifted

We lost contact and now it's just too awkward

removable skins piled high
        to be spun
        to be tumbled
        to be folded
        to be put away

I don't think I would worry if his ex was in town

microwave and oven timers sing
        voices not as sweet as mom's

But then again, they had a bad break-up

warm waterfall cascading in a tile cubicle
echoing words of the day

He shouldn't worry, or be mad at me now

flannel sheet envelope
unwinds tangled lobes of a callused brain
cradles a Chihuahua at my feet

I'm just going to have to call him back

hop-scotch to tomorrow

'Til We Meet Again

Say goodbye
>	to lazy river days.
>>		Racin' kayaks to the concrete slab
>>		in your granddaddy's old rock quarry
>>		so you could climb up rusty i-beams.
>>		You tyin' my kayak to a tree with a rope
>>		when I didn't have an anchor to keep me
>>		from floatin' away with the breeze.
>>		Or me layin' out across your moccasin boat
>>		singin' old hymns, my head on your folded shirt
>>		and a line in the water waitin' on a cork dittle.
>>		You jumpin' over the side to swim under
>>		and pop up with water drippin' off the brim
>>		of that smelly old camouflage hat onto my hand
>>		and kissin' my ring, with water tricklin' down my arm.

Say goodbye
>	to four-wheeler trails.
>>		Ridin' out to the water's edge just to watch
>>		fish break surface as the sun grows darker and heavier,
>>		until the crickets sing and frogs bellow melodies.
>>		Pushin' through the weeds to find the honeysuckle
>>		smelled from far away just to bite the end and sip
>>		nature's sweetness before puttin' the flower in my hair.
>>		Goin' down to the boat landin' and docks for a swim
>>		or climbin' up the ladder to swing out on a rope
>>		tied to a tree and droppin' in way over our heads.
>>		Sittin' in the cow pasture to watch planes come and go
>>		until their lights blend in with the stars we dream on
>>		and wish we could set up a tent and never have to leave.

Say goodbye
>	to the one thing that was made only once and never again.
>	Once it's lost it's gone for good. It constantly changes,
>	but is constantly the same. It stays with you when you leave it.

Black

Velvet is the engulfing darkness
night embraces about its victims.
Black tires leave black streaks
on asphalt as crickets sing
eighth notes in the shadows.
Moonlight dances on the onyx
surface of the water until
a black dress and tuxedo
are left on the dock as two
lost souls plunge into uncertainty
and laugh at death.

Go ahead, honey

Dare to dream in his direction,
but look longer than a glance
and I'll close your eyes.
I don't feel threatened,
I just refuse to be disrespected.
So find another cold shoulder
to take home, sleep tight tonight.
You'll never leave lipstick
"I love you's" on his collar,
smell his cologne
linger on your pillow,
know how his hair feels
between your fingers, feel
his breath send chills
down your neck,
or hear his first words
of every morning.

Try to flirt without
making me take notice.
Just know I've had my fair share
of parking lot and bathroom brawls,
but I don't open hand slap or pull hair.
I'll laugh in your face if you do.
So that's at least one thing
you ain't woman enough for.

Smile at him once and you'll choke
on your own teeth.
I'm not blind, I know women
want what I have.
I see it in your eyes when it's me
on his arm entering a room.

Wink at him once and I'll beat
the ugly right out of you.
I'm not deaf, I hear the sighs
as he walks near to order a beer.

Say something you might think
is smart or witty
and you'll only be able
to hiss like a possum.

I'm not stupid, I know
you'd take a chance
for a lifetime of pain
I'm willing to inflict
with just a smile and nod.
I'll educate you with the right
hand of fellowship. You'll drop
like a tater sack, limp and empty
of thoughts to try something
so foolish again,
just like all the rest,
even his ex and my own cousin.
You'll look and feel
like a tractor ran over you
with the plows attached.

Dance with me

in the yellow beams of your truck's headlights, help
me sing along as the radio plays our favorite song

in the green arms of a weeping willow tree
barely brushing ground, let them tangle
around us as the moon peaks through

in black and white with spotlight on us,
our guests watch as we sway back and forth
with our eyes closed and our feet touching

all night long to the same old sweet love songs
until white candles melt clothes to the floor

in the soft blue glow of a hallway nightlight
outside a nursery to the tinkle of a lullaby

in an empty house when it's just us again
by the fireplace, let the red flames show
thin lines settling in around our eyes

to the melody rain plays on an old tin roof
when it's hard to stand, hold me close
to see your face and trace the silver in my hair

Dinner for Two

He held the door open for her
      without putting his hand
      on the small of her back.

How many this evening?

Dinner for two, he says looking
      around the crowded room.

In one dimly lit corner
      a young woman cries
      shaking her head yes,
      a little white box
      held open before her
      in trembling hands.

At a bright center table
      a cake is brought out
      to a small child
      in a pointed hat clapping
      and singing.

In a side booth situated along
      the wall an old couple
      sit by a window, the man
      pointing to the stars
      and holding her hand.

I have something to tell you, he says
      looking through his wine glass.
So do I, she says with a girlish smile.

She sees him look at his left hand,
then quickly put it under the table.

She thinks of their first date,
a picnic at Union Point Park
and a carriage ride down town
to see the Christmas decorations.
They stopped here for a Styrofoam cup
of apple cider he scratched their initials on.

She thinks of how he proposed
in this restaurant and how
he had taken the time to rent
the entire upstairs and have it
decorated with flowers and candles.
A small band played in the corner.

She smoothes her skirt as she works
up the courage to tell him her news.
She did her best to look good for him
on such a special night as this,
another one to add to their memories.

This whole time he twists his
wedding band around his finger
with his hands under the table.
Then she notices they were
not holding hers and that instead
of staring back into her eyes
he is just blankly looking at her.

Is something wrong? she asks,
fearing he is not feeling well.

He fidgets with his tie, sips
his wine, and clears his throat.
I've met someone new, he says
      and walks away without
      saying happy anniversary,
his wedding band left spinning
on the table in front of her.

Shall I box this up for you, ma'am?

No thank you, I'm eating for two.

Proposal of a Simple Country Girl

Darlin' I'll never be a model or millionaire,
      the epitome of any man's dreams.
I'm only human, no princess by far,
      just a simple country girl
from a town full of rivers and fields
      where spot lights replace stop lights.
Everybody speaks in a slow Southern drawl,
      every conversation
      has a "bless your heart".
Summers are hotter than a whore in church
      with a ten dollar date in the choir,
and winters are colder than a witch's titty
      in a brass bra doin' push-ups in the snow.
Cool John Deere-green grass
      always feels better under bare feet.
You can drink homemade moonshine
      and wine of any flavor.
Cow tippin', 'possum kickin', and frog giggin'
      are late-night sports.
Hearin' Mama yellin' your full name,
      wooden spoon in one hand,
      Bible in the other,
always brings about a wild-eyed
      deer-in-the-headlights look.
Trucks are bigger and cars are faster
      thanks to illegal parts,
everybody has a boat and four-wheeler
      just for Saturday play.
Everybody works hard at least
      five days a week
and fills Sundays with church
      and big family dinners.
Grandma always says if you lose
      something then it was never
      really yours to begin with,
so whoever leaves here

and never comes back
never saw all these things
        that'll always hold me here
'cause home is where the heart is,
        and a tree can't grow
        away from its roots.
I'm half redneck woman
        and half southern belle
        dependin' on the day
in busted and worn jeans and a t-shirt
        or floor-length gown
        and four inch heels.
I'm as pure and sweet as honey-suckle
        right off the bush.
I can tell you the difference
        between a hissy fit
        and a conniption
        and which is worse.
I can handle any type of gun
        and will collect them
        as long as NRA is still around.
I can throw a ball hard as a man,
        thanks to many years of softball.
I can coax a baby to sleep
        with a sway and a song
        thanks to many years in the choir.
I can make sweet iced tea good enough
        to make you wanna slap the preacher.
Darlin', I know what it means
        to "commence" to do something,
"squawlin'" is either intense cryin'
        or the sound a bald tire makes,
and that openin' up a can
        of whoop ass is a force
        not to be reckoned with.
I have a belt with my name
        and huge buckle on it I wear
        with my cowboy hat and boots.

I consider goin' to a baseball game,
       mud bog, tractor pull, or drag strip
       a certifiable date.
I have been know to "relocate"
       a few road signs in my time.
I like Pepsis with peanuts in them,
       a Slim Jim or nab on the side.
I like my coffee like I like my men,
       strong but not too rich.
I like standin' out in those hot summer rains
       when each drop turns to swirls
       of steam dancin' off your skin.
Some folks may think I'm just another nobody
       from nowhere goin' nowhere.
But I'm gonna be a doctor one day
       and I hope to heal
       a lot more than sickness.
I'm gonna write a book of poetry
       about the simple things
       I'll always love.
That is if the Lord's willin'
       and the creek don't rise.
'Cause Daddy always says
       the only free thing in life
       is your name and it's only
       worth what you make it.
Darlin' I'll never be anyone special,
       just another name carved in stone.
But I can give you a promise
       that'll always be priceless to me.
I'll be there every night by your side
       in dreamful slumber,
and the nights you lie awake
       talkin' up the sun.
I'll be there every mornin'
       to Eskimo kiss you awake
and cover you in caresses to protect
       and warm you through the day.

I'll be there every day just a holler
        or phone call away
and heal your troubles with a lazy smile
        by tellin' you I love you
        "a bushel and a peck
        and a hug around the neck".
The road ahead of me looks a lot
        like the one behind
        that's been guidin' me through,
unlined and unpaved, just dirt and gravel
        with potholes sometimes
        filled with rain.
But if you think you can handle
        this simple country girl
        and all that implies,
then we can barefoot this ol' road
        together one step at a time.

White

Driving past the old Brock Mill Pond
the other day I noticed a new sign up
and that it was finally holding water,
white-capping over the new concrete,
but I think the building's still
condemned. They'll probably paint
it white once it's restored, more bright
and refreshing than the gray. I saw ducks
and geese were in for winter,
pecking at stale white bread crumbs
at the feet of cypresses and willows,
Spanish moss falling to the ground.
This same scene has been painted
many times and has seen its share
of generations of picnicking couples,
even my parents when they were young.
It's perfect for my bridal portraits.

Just past there is the old Trenton Church
where my parents grew up, met, wed,
and Christened me. I noticed someone
had started painting the two-hundred
year-old siding where it had been peeling.
I was glad to see they kept it white, even
the bell tower where my daddy used to sit
every New Year's Eve ringing in
another year. No other color would suite
it, and as far as I know that's the only
color it's ever been. I couldn't help
but wish it were big enough to hold
all the guests we had to invite, but it was sure
big enough to hold a lot of memories.

I'd love to buy it some day
just to restore it so it'll never crumble
like the many types of congregations
it's seen come and go over centuries.
Maybe I'd plant a rose garden beside it
with flowers of every kind and color,
especially white to match the church.
I'll take another photo on the front steps.

After my drive through the past, I went back
to where we had been painting together
in the master bedroom of our future home.
It may not be new, but at least it's ours.
A few hours later I was in white primer
polka-dotted sweats and T-shirt from trim work
with the radio playing in the living room,
singing along to the old songs Mama taught
me from childhood I didn't know I remembered.
I was thinking about how things change,
and how they always stay the same.
He asked if I needed a break, but I said I was fine,
so he took my paintbrush and set it aside.
He led me by the hand into the living room to dance
and asked what color I wanted in the bedroom.
I think I'd like to just keep it white.

PART III

gold dust

can you compare
    a choir of angels
        ten thousand fold
            to your mama's voice
                as she sings
                    Amazing Grace
            and runs her fingers
        through your hair
    until you drift
beyond childhood
                can you compare
        a star's glisten
      to the shimmer
    off a diamond ring
or the glitter
in your makeup
    transferred in a kiss
        on your daddy's cheek
            as he gives you away
                to the one you love
can you compare
    the moon's blink
        through window blinds
            to a shadow's dance
                of silhouettes
                a candle's flame
            flickers on the wall
        the first night
    in your new
home of your own

can you compare
the engulfing warmth
of the sun's peek
to an embrace
and your lover's wink
as he holds
open the door
and you walk out
on the first day
of your career

can you look
out the window
of a hospital room
beyond the clouds
'til the sky
is no longer blue
and feel God smile
when you look
into your newborn's
huckleberry eyes

Games Children Play

Our children don't know
what we say to each other
when they're not around,
they only know what we tell them.
They can't possibly understand
complexity of adult affairs.
They play their games
of hide and seek and I spy
not knowing there are things
to hide from or seek out
and new things to discover.
They play house not knowing
that it's a mirror image of life
and that nothing is what it seems.
They question without knowing
the source of their inquiry.
Maybe it's memories in dreams,
maybe something seen on TV.
Either way they get it all from us.

cheese doodle handprints

on neon bathing suits
dripping on concrete
when halfway folded up
lawn chairs were cars
with beach towels
for a rag top easily removed
to make a convertible
with a paper plate
steering wheel
and a coke bottle shifter
those Quaker Neck
summers by the pool

when Barbie was recon
with GI Joe
and Ken was her brother
houseplants were jungles
where they'd get caught
in dust storms
and chemical attacks
when left out on stake-outs

on army green t-shirts
grass-stained blue jeans
spying with binoculars
from grandma's dogwood
armed with only golf club guns
baseball bat bazookas
and baseball hand grenades
to ward off any boys
who thought girls
shouldn't play with them
but you never seemed to mind

Times

There have been times
when we could have fought
each other
but more times
we would have fought
for each other;

when we've cried
tears of happiness
and of sadness
for each other
but more
with each other;

when misunderstandings
and distance
separated us
until learning
people don't always
change with miles.

We've seen each other
at worst and best times
without judgment
falling apart
or falling in love;

success and failure
never boasted
nor masked
because truth hides
in the eyes
like the things we let slip
when we think
no one's looking.

There will be times
when communication
may falter
slip through
calendar cracks;

it's not just the big days
like graduations
weddings and births
but the regular day hey
that truly tests time;

when we need a smile
on a familiar face
of a longtime friend
to say remember when.

Red, White, & Blue

It's in the red
of every muscle
flexed to fight
and the river
streaks in eyes
from the loss
of sleep at night.
It's in the passion
felt in each
blood drop shed.

It's in the white
of the knuckles
clenched in a fist
and the hands
folded in prayer.
It's in the salt
lost in each
sweat drop shed.

It's in the blue
of every bruise
appearing through skin
and the oceans
separating kin.
It's in the water
formed into puddles
of tear drops shed.

No matter what
the colors mean
they fly for freedom
for you and me.

Death

A single cigarette burning out in a cold metal ashtray
an orange glow slowly growing dim
turning to ashes until completely consumed
by the darkness it once pierced.

YOMEMOM: You're Still Here

I close my eyes and see your face,
  scenes of times shared in
movie theatres watching silly teen movies
  like "She's All That" when you were
  disappointed at the end when it didn't show
  naked Freddie Prinze Jr. after
  he threw the soccer ball to the girl;
shopping malls where we'd people-watch,
  check out guys, buy things we didn't need;
ball parks where I heard a familiar Philly accent
  cheering me on from the bleachers,
  telling people there was nothing I couldn't do.

I cup my ears and hear your laugh,
  loud, raspy, and hearty
  like whatever brought it on
  was the funniest thing you'd ever heard;
the way you called everyone "Hon",
  family, friends, and strangers alike
  as if you'd known them all your like;
how it sounded when I taught you to say "ya'll",
  you'd even move your jaw in a circle
  to draw it out so it at least looked right;
the time you asked if it was ducks that made the noises
  after a rain, we laughed and said yeah
  the little green kind that perch on windows.

Ashes to ashes, dust to dust
  that's all people say is left,
but I see more, because you're still here
  in your grandchildren.
You are the twinkling laughter in their eyes
  when their imaginations
  run wild with make-believe,
and when they grow wide

with curiosity after learning
some new exciting thing,
but especially when they remember
something fun they once
shared only with you.
They always addressed you like
Yo, Memom! with a smile,
so your license plate read.
It stood displayed next to you
as loved ones gathered
in your name.
It's how you are best remembered,
those kids were your everything.

What made her eyes change
from blue to green like yours?
She looks more like you everyday.
She says, *Stars are angels,
my Memom is the brightest.*
What made him gaze in curious wonder
at the fireman helmets on the wall?
He grows strong like you everyday.
He says, *I'm left-handed,
just like my Memom.*

Their hearts form questions
their minds can't comprehend.
One day they will need answers
to what, how, who, and why
yet some will never come.
We hide your things,
remove all evidence
So they never remember
to ask what happened
to the toys they kept at your house
now black reminders of a day
burned into their past
melted into their future.

We tell them stories
     so they'll never forget
     who you were,
who will always be
     as long as we remember.

The hardest thing for me is to look at them
     knowing they didn't have
     enough time with you.
So if to you there was nothing I couldn't do,
then I'll make this promise
     that they'll always know you,
you'll live on in everything they'll ever do.

Unveil Reality

Unlearn me of the hurts of my yesterday
    when I knew not the confusion of pain.
Return me to the innocence ignorance gives
    before unwanted knowledge tangled
    my chambered heart with my lobed brain.
Unleash this internally biting pit bull anger
    from stress unanticipated adulthood brings.
Unburn from my ears the scars left behind
    from inaudible screams that haunt my dreams.
Unscar the tissues of soaked saline insanity
    extract the ducts or dehydrate them
    to brittle numbness that crumbles.
Abort me as the unexpected everyday miracle,
    detach me so that I may never
    know of inhuman cruelty.
Revive the compassion murdered by murder
    and unthaw the heart froze in death's breath.
No I'll not pretty it any longer for my own sake
    but look into the mirror that hides the key
    I must salvage and unsoot to fit the lock of truth.
My own shadow dare not follow where I must go
    for there is no light to cast it in the depths
    of darkness death only knows.
Yes I'll stare death in the face, deny it,
    defy its lies with words of immortal truth.
Wake me from this dream that is my reality so that
    I may learn, hear, and love through life again.

Christmas is Gone

Ribbons and bows, trashed
with red and green papers,

snatched from beneath
new "holiday" trees

still dressed up evergreen,
some now hung from ceilings.

Family dinners are out of hand
with feuds and spiked egg nog.

Greetings in stores and cards
less common, colder

with X's in place of Christ
on non-recyclable paper,

killing more trees. Fake smiles
and slogans telling prices

for items jacked up 25%
on sale 10% off this time only.

Cartoon-themed figurines
are characters in manger scenes,

who knows what a shepherd
or wise man looks like anymore.

Fewer waves with hopeful wishes,
but more obscenities in traffic.

The reason for the season
is greed and grief given

for those fortunate or less,
homeless or wealthy.

Just food and presents devoured
without thanks or I love you's.

No carols sang or story read
now for "happy holidays".

A Sonnet to My Great Grandma Effie,
Who First Brought My Family to Church

There was a woman I wish I had known.
I've seen her pictures. Mama looks like her
when she was young. There's an heirloom I own,
a bracelet to wear when pictures are blurred.
At times her footsteps were heard on the floor,
come down the aisle and stop right by her pew.
While cleaning at the church behind shut door,
I heard a female alto echo through.
Though all alone I knew who it must be.
She often visits time to time like in
my Mama's smile, a wind's whisper to me,
and sometimes in my music box's tinkling.
Great grandma Effie, I promise today
to keep a rocking chair for you to sway.

Close-lined

It hung in the air
        a translucent gray cloud
engulfing the distance between them
like someone close-lined
        and caught on the cord.

Don't worry I won't tell her
        she says and returns to washing
dirty dishes with blurred eyes
        staring out the window.

It's because I respect her
        he says and hangs
his head so that the shadow
        of his hat hides his red face.

She'll be home tomorrow
        she says and looks
to the empty space
        a red car will soon fill.

Then I'll quit tonight
        he says and grabs his chest
while an antique lighter falls
        from a white-knuckled fist.

It hung in the air
        a haunting late night ring
engulfing the distance between them
like someone close-lined
        and caught on the cord.

Thanks for Your Son

Thanks for your son.
Without him I wouldn't
live today.
Words cried in a prayer
at the foot of the cross
hanging on the church wall
over memories relived
of a night when she stumbled
in to find that empty alter,
and after reading a verse aloud
through tear-blurred vision
removed the gun from her temple.
That was the same night
he came in to fix the plumbing
and held her there, humming
Amazing Grace, just a stranger
who later became her husband.

Thanks for your son.
Without him I wouldn't
live today.
Words a daughter-in-law
says aloud to the headstone
of a woman she never knew,
and places beside it a porcelain
figure of an angel watching
over children on a bridge.
A tear falls on the hand
rested on her stomach
as she says congratulations,
and wishes she and the baby
had a chance to know her.
This was the first time
she had come here

without her husband,
but this was something
she had to do for herself.

Thanks for your son.
Without him I wouldn't
live today.
Words a mother reads
in a note inside her door.
She presses it
in the family Bible
on the desk between
a triangular frame
holding a folded flag
and a blurred picture
with lip-prints on the glass.
She noticed how much
he favored his grandmother,
he and his father had her smile.
Not even her husband's
strong shoulders
could console her now.

www.ingramcontent.com/pod-product-compliance
Lightning Source LLC
Chambersburg PA
CBHW030523290526
45786CB00004B/1588